Cheery

THE TRUE ADVENTURES OF A CHIRICAHUA LEOPARD FROG

BY ELIZABETH W. DAVIDSON

ILLUSTRATED BY MICHAEL HAGELBERG

Little Five Star

A DIVISION OF FIVE STAR PUBLICATIONS, INC., CHANDLER, ARIZONA

Text Copyright © 2011
Elizabeth W. Davidson

Illustrations Copyright © 2011
Michael Hagelberg

Linda F. Radke, President
Five Star Publications, Inc.
PO Box 6698
Chandler, AZ 85246-6698
480-940-8182
www.CheeryAFrogsTale.com

Library of Congress Cataloging-in-Publication Data

Davidson, Elizabeth W.
Cheery : a frog's tale / by Elizabeth W. Davidson.
       p. cm.

ISBN-13: 978-1-58985-025-5
ISBN-10: 1-58985-025-4
eISBN: 978-1-58985-026-2

1. Leopard frogs–Juvenile literature.
2. Endangered species–Juvenile literature. I. Title.
QL668.E27D38 2011
597.8'92–dc22
                          2010049238

Electronic edition provided by

eStarPublish.com
www.eStarPublish.com
the eDivision of Five Star Publications, Inc.

Printed in the United States of America
Illustrated and designed by Michael Hagelberg

THIS BOOK IS DEDICATED TO OUR GRANDSON, JOSEPH JEREMIAH DAVIDSON—E.D.

Acknowledgments

I am grateful for the many useful suggestions from authors Brooke Bessesen and Conrad Storad, and anonymous reviewers. My husband, Joseph Davidson, provided important support for the writing and publication of the book. Michael Hagelberg exhibited great artistic talents and hard work in producing the illustrations. The rapid and professional work of Five Star Publications was extremely helpful. Without the strong encouragement from many friends and colleagues, especially Robert Brucker, Marci Welton and Marj Townsend, this book would not have been accomplished. This book came about from experiences I've had tutoring second and third-graders through All-Star Kids Tutoring Program. The Phoenix Zoo permitted us to observe their captive breeding program for the Chiricahua Leopard Frogs. I am also grateful for the financial support this project received from Arizona Game and Fish Division Heritage Grant Program.

ELIZABETH W. DAVIDSON

Heritage Fund

My name is Cheery.

I'm a Chiricahua (Cheer-a-cow-ah) Leopard Frog tadpole.
I'm sometimes called a pollywog.

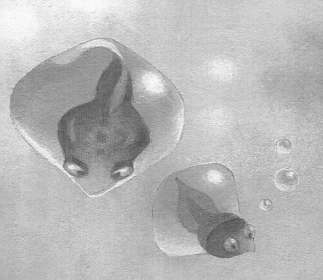

I woke up today curled inside a gooey egg.
I'm surrounded by hundreds of other gooey eggs here
in the pond. Each of these eggs has one of my brothers
or sisters inside. We wiggle and twist for hours.
When we burst free of our eggs, we begin swimming.

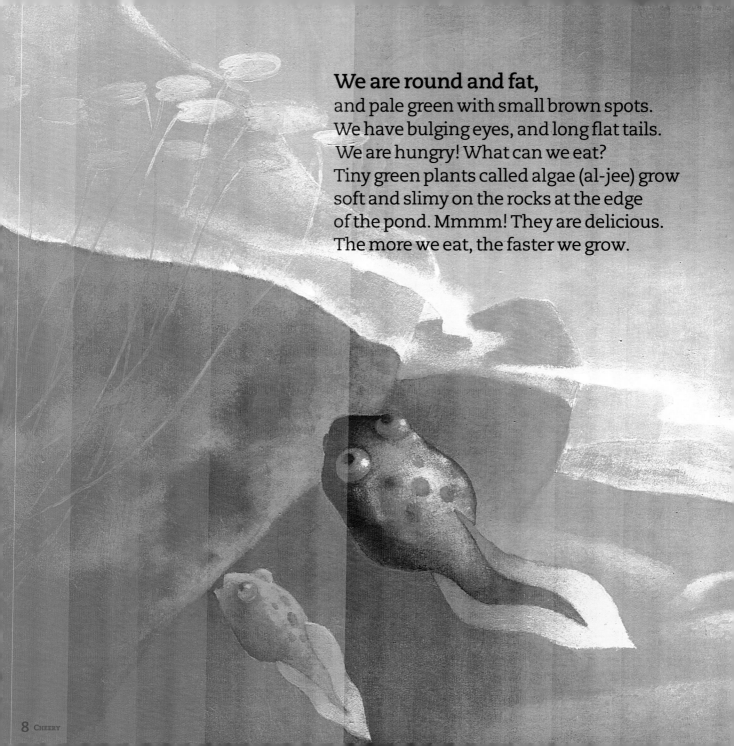

We are round and fat,
and pale green with small brown spots.
We have bulging eyes, and long flat tails.
We are hungry! What can we eat?
Tiny green plants called algae (al-jee) grow
soft and slimy on the rocks at the edge
of the pond. Mmmm! They are delicious.
The more we eat, the faster we grow.

Our small pond is nestled in the shade
of mountain pine trees. Warmed by the sun,
birds sing and dragonflies buzz around the
pond. In the evening, deer and elk often come
to drink from the pond.

A wise Chiricahua Leopard Frog is sitting at
the muddy edge of the pond. Wise Old Frog,
as all my Chiricahua friends call him, tells us
that during one long hot summer when
he was young, his home pond dried up.
He hopped through the forest until he
found our pond and made it his home.

We trust Wise Old Frog because he has
lived here for many years, and because
he warns us when danger is near.

SNAP! All of a sudden, big sharp claws are trying to grab me!

It has eight legs and sure moves fast! "It is a crayfish," says Wise Old Frog, "and very dangerous!" I quickly hide under a rock.

SPLASH! Wow, I just saw a huge frog! His mouth is bigger than I am!
Wise Old Frog says it is a bullfrog and to be careful. He says the bullfrog
might eat us and, if we get too close, he might give us a deadly disease.
All night long the bullfrog calls, GO ROUND, GO ROUND.
I am very afraid of the bullfrog. I swim away as fast as I can.

Wise Old Frog says someone brought
the bullfrog and the crayfish from
far away and put them in our pond.
Why? What were they thinking?

All summer long, I eat lots of the delicious green algae
in the pond. As the days pass, I see I'm slowly beginning to change
shape. First, I grow long back legs and feet. Next, I grow front legs.
Finally, I lose my tail. Now I look like Wise Old Frog!

I curl up my back legs and jump as high as I can,
right out of the pond and onto the land.

I begin exploring the edge of the pond. There is a cricket! I catch it with one quick jump. YUMMY! No more green algae for me. Pretty soon, my friends and I are gobbling up mosquitoes, beetles and spiders. We grow fatter and fatter every day. When evening comes, we hop back into the pond to spend the night. We sing our song all night long– SNORE SNORE SNORE.

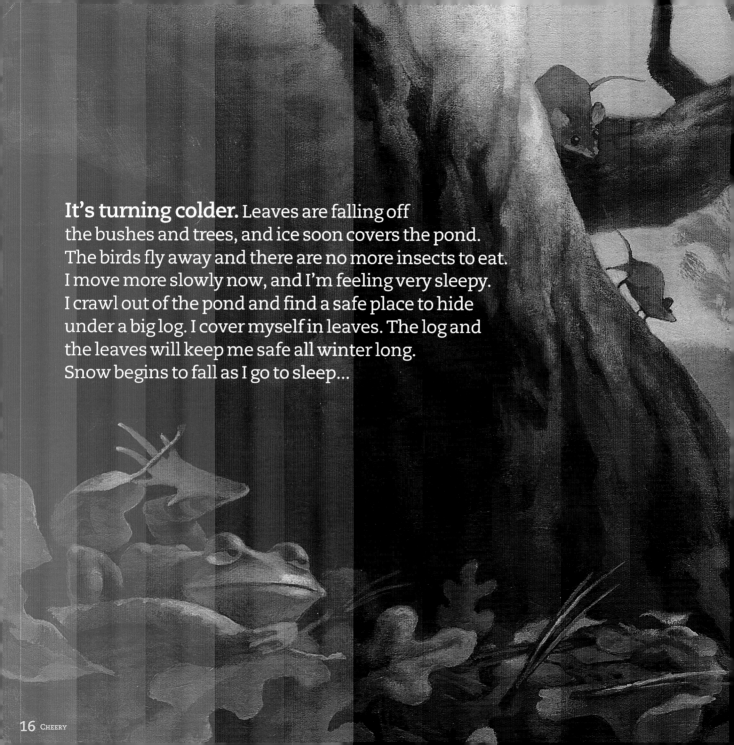

It's turning colder. Leaves are falling off
the bushes and trees, and ice soon covers the pond.
The birds fly away and there are no more insects to eat.
I move more slowly now, and I'm feeling very sleepy.
I crawl out of the pond and find a safe place to hide
under a big log. I cover myself in leaves. The log and
the leaves will keep me safe all winter long.
Snow begins to fall as I go to sleep…

...after many months

go by, it begins to get warmer.
The snow melts, and the bushes
and trees beside the pond make
new green leaves. I begin to
stir in my bed under the log.
Spring is here! I hear birds
singing and I see butterflies
are floating around my log.
I hop around the pond
to find my friends.
But wait—where are
all my friends? I can't
find them anywhere.

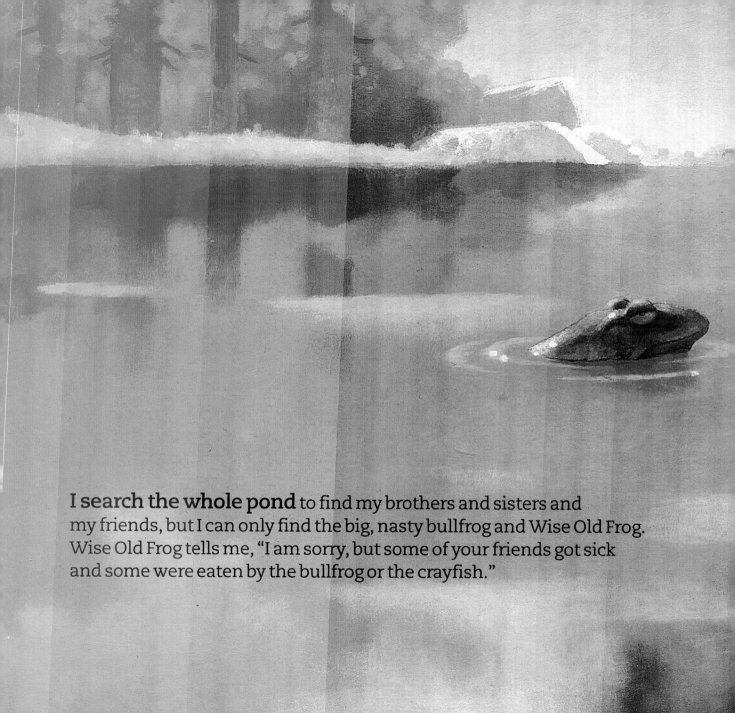

I search the whole pond to find my brothers and sisters and my friends, but I can only find the big, nasty bullfrog and Wise Old Frog. Wise Old Frog tells me, "I am sorry, but some of your friends got sick and some were eaten by the bullfrog or the crayfish."

I am so lonely and sad.

Later that night, rain begins to fall—first a few drops and then a huge thunderstorm. I sit out in the rain and try singing my funny little song: SNORE, SNORE, SNORE.

I hope someone will hear me. For the longest time, no one answers me.

Wait! I hear something.
It sounds like
SNORE SNORE SNORE.
It's coming from the far corner
of the pond. Could that really be
another Chiricahua frog singing?

I hop over and there he is! He is
a beautiful light brown color,
with dark brown spots, and bright
black eyes. My new friend has
a sharp pointy nose and striped legs,
and he can swallow a dragonfly
in a single bite!

The next evening,
my new friend and I see
a light moving along the edge
of the pond. Our eyes glow
brightly when the light hits us.
Suddenly a net falls over us!

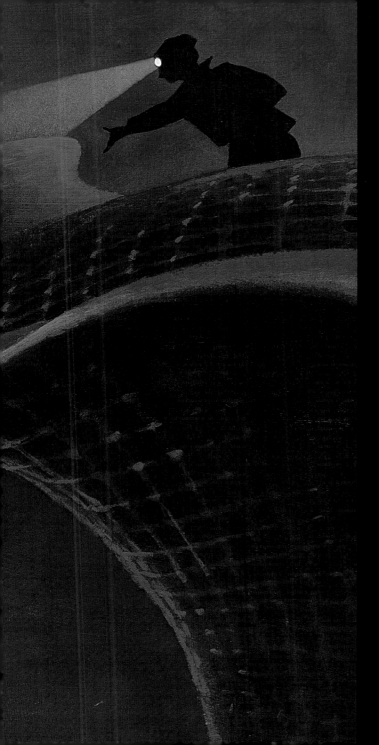

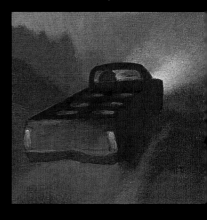

Without any warning,
we are yanked out of the
pond, dropped into a
bucket, and put in
the back of a truck.
All night long, we jiggle
down the mountain.
When daylight comes,
we are finally carried ou
of the truck.

We hear strange
roaring, cackling,
and trumpeting sounds
all around us.
What is this place?
We have no idea!

Then we hear them:
SNORE, SNORE, SNORE.
There are more
Chiricahua
Leopard Frogs here!

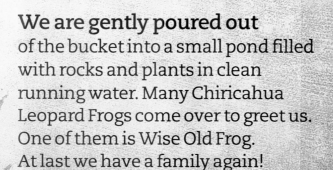

We are gently poured out
of the bucket into a small pond filled
with rocks and plants in clean
running water. Many Chiricahua
Leopard Frogs come over to greet us.
One of them is Wise Old Frog.
At last we have a family again!

Wise Old Frog says we are in a zoo.
He tells us it's a place where people
will love and care for us every day.
Just as he says that, a kind lady
brings us lots of crickets to feast on.

As the days and weeks
pass by, we make lots of eggs
in sticky masses on plants
in the water. The zoo ladies
carefully move the eggs to
a quiet place and watch over
them. About two weeks later
hundreds of new tadpoles appear!

The zoo ladies feed the tadpoles
every day. They grow and grow.
In about three months, the tadpoles
lose their tails, grow legs, and
become frogs just like us!

Then one wonderful afternoon,
the zoo people take us in the truck again
back to our old pond under the pine trees.
While we were at the zoo, people had removed
all the bullfrogs and crayfish from the pond.
Now it's safe for us to live here.

We jump in, hopping and splashing.
We sing SNORE SNORE SNORE
all night long. And I'm not
lonely anymore!

The Chiricahua Leopard Frog and Amphibian Decline

Amphibians (including frogs, salamanders and a rare animal called a caecilian) are disappearing around the world. One out of three species world-wide is either threatened with extinction or has already disappeared forever. This story focuses on one such amphibian, the Chiricahua Leopard Frog (scientific name *Rana chiricahuensis*), which originally inhabited hundreds of ponds and streams in the mountains and valleys of east-central and south-eastern Arizona and northern Mexico.

Sadly, Chiricahua Leopard Frogs have disappeared from more than 80% of the sites where they once lived. They are now restricted to human-made cattle tanks as well as a few streams and springs. They are listed as a "Threatened Species" by the US Fish and Wildlife Service, which means they are in danger of extinction. It is believed the decline in numbers of the Chiricahua Leopard Frog is due to a combination of factors: a fungus disease, introduced predators (fish, crayfish and bullfrogs), loss of habitat, and drought.

The US Fish and Wildlife Service, Arizona Game and Fish Department, and the US Department of the Interior have developed a recovery plan for these frogs that includes encouraging landowners to maintain ponds where they live, removal of introduced predators, and—as told in this story— captive breeding at zoos and parks with the goal of returning the frogs to safe habitats in the future.

Many other species of amphibians from around the world are being protected and reared by conservation organizations in a project called the Amphibian Ark. We hope all children will come to love and protect these and other amphibians in the future.

Further information can be found at AmphibiaWeb (amphibiaweb.org); U.S. Fish and Wildlife Service (ecos.fws.gov/) ; Amphibians of Arizona (www.reptilesofaz.org); and other sites.

PHOTO BY DR. PHIL ROSEN, UNIVERSITY OF ARIZONA.

We wish them well!

What happened to the Chiricahua Leopard frogs? Many of their ponds and streams dried up or were drained for agriculture, and people brought in crayfish and bullfrogs that can eat frogs. Recently a serious disease that can be carried by bullfrogs and salamanders has reduced their numbers even more. This disease has been found in many places around the world where amphibians have gone missing, including the Chiricahua Leopard Frogs. Around one third of all amphibians in the world are now extinct or in danger of becoming extinct. (To go extinct means that it is gone forever; for example, dinosaurs are extinct.)

Why should we care if frogs are going missing? Amphibians, and especially frogs, are important in the "food web". They eat insects that bite us, and they serve as food for fish, birds and other animals. Some kinds of frogs are used in classrooms to teach how our bodies are put together, and to do experiments. We are beginning to learn that some frogs have chemicals in their skin that we may use as antibiotics to help cure some diseases. And they are fun to watch!

Froggy Facts

What is an amphibian? Amphibians are animals with backbones (vertebrates) just like us. But they generally live part or all of their life in the water, lay eggs in the water, and can breathe through their skin as well as with their noses and lungs!

How many are there? It is estimated that there are between 4000 and 5000 different species (kinds) of amphibians in the world. There are about 230 in the United States.

Are frogs the same as lizards and snakes? No! Lizards and snakes are reptiles. They are also vertebrates, but they have scales and live mostly on land. Scientists have placed reptiles and amphibians in the same Phylum (*Vertebrata*), but frogs are in the Class *Amphibia* while reptiles are in the Class *Reptilia*.

What amphibians may we find in the wild? The most common ones are frogs (which are usually close to water), toads (that live mostly on land), and salamanders (that have long tails and are often mistaken for lizards). There is also a very rare amphibian called a caecilian which looks a lot like a snake and generally lives underground.

Where does the Chiricahua Leopard Frog live? Cheery used to live in many places in Arizona, New Mexico, and northern Mexico. But sadly, now the Chiricahua frogs live only in a few small ponds in these areas. Chiricahua frogs raised in zoos have recently been taken back to some ponds in Arizona.

Curriculum Guide

A book should be shared with a child numerous times. At each reading your child learns more vocabulary and by following good reading strategies, your child will begin the journey to understanding literature. Sharing a book is a very enjoyable experience and at the same time your child will be learning plot structure, sequence and characterization.

Follow these three stages of reading and use one or more of the strategies each time you share the book.

During Reading:

Keep count or keep names of all the animals mentioned in the story.

Pronounce each vocabulary word as you come to it in the story.

Cheery exhibits many different moods from happy to sad. Make a face which mirrors each mood.

Why is Cheery afraid of the crayfish and the bullfrog?

There are many exciting parts to Cheery's story. Which is the most important action? *(being scooped up in nets.)*

After Reading:

How did the bullfrog and the crayfish get into the pond *(Page 12)*? What has that done to the environment of the pond?

Can you think of other times someone put the wrong thing into an environment? *(oil spills, industrial waste, car exhaust, plastic bags.)*

Who is looking out for the Chiricahua Leopard Frogs? Scientists at Arizona Game and Fish Department, the US Fish and Wildlife Service and universities watch over the frogs in their ponds. The Phoenix Zoo has raised the new frogs who have been returned to the wild.

Hear the sound of the bullfrog and the Chiricahua Leopard Frog by using an internet search or visit http://www.allaboutfrogs.org.

Learn more about the Chiricahua Leopard Frog: www.fws.gov/southwest/es/arizona/CLF.htm.

Use Play-Doh® or clay to model the stages of development of a frog. Use a small round ball for the egg. Use another small ball with a small pointed tail for the tadpole. Then make a larger ball with the beginnings of head, legs and arms. Finally roll the largest ball and attach a fully developed head and appendages.

Soak some large pearl tapioca in a small bowl of warm water. Let it sit for a few minutes and then the tapioca will resemble small frog eggs.

Read about the Amphibian Ark Project: www.amphibianark.org.

About the Author

Elizabeth W. Davidson received her doctorate in entomology from Ohio State University where she studied the interactions between insects and bacteria. Her research in this field is now being used worldwide to help control mosquitoes and black flies.

In recent years, she has focused her research on the diseases of amphibians and has worked in collaboration with scientists from around the globe. Her work and that of her colleagues has shown that amphibians are disappearing at an alarming rate in countries all over the world (nearly half of all species could become extinct during our lifetimes). Dr. Davidson and her colleagues are working to isolate the various causes of these population declines and to help preserve these fascinating creatures. Her laboratory, for example, found a highly pathogenic virus causing die-offs of the endangered Sonoran tiger salamander (*Ambystoma tigrinum stebbinsi*).

Dr. Davidson and her husband, Dr. Joseph Davidson, have been at Arizona State University since 1973. Their son, Scott, is a middle school science teacher. The Davidson's enjoy international travel and outdoor adventures. In her spare time, Dr. Davidson has tutored second and third grade students in reading through the All Star Kids Tutoring program, an experience which led to the writing of *Cheery: the true adventures of a Chiricahua Leopard Frog.*

Photo by Jacob Mayfield

About the Illustrator

Michael Hagelberg couldn't make up his mind what to be when he grew up. He had a strong affinity for science and natural history, but art was also tempting. He eventually gave in to art.

He began his career as a designer with agency and freelance work after graduating from Northern Arizona University, but the desire to combine science and art soon took him into educational publication. He became creative director, designer and illustrator of Arizona State University's award winning *Research* magazine. His graphic design and illustration has been recognized by awards from the University and College Designers Association, International Association of Business Communicators and Council for Advancement and Support of Education.

Today he illustrates for magazine and book publishers, as well as developing fine art and stamina for bicycling.

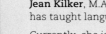

ABOUT THE CREATOR OF THE CURRICULUM GUIDE

Jean Kilker, M.A. (English), M.Ed. (Technology), NBCT (National Board Certification), has taught language arts, reading and science.

Currently, she is a Teacher-Librarian and former Follett Librarian of the Year. She is a member of the Public Library Advisory Board and co-chair of the State Teacher-Librarian Organization. She also teaches and writes curriculum at the university level for continuing teacher education in ESL, elementary language arts, reading and librarianship. In addition, she has received grants and awards that benefit the students where she teaches.

A native of Phoenix, Arizona, she and her husband live in Litchfield Park, Arizona, and keep in touch with their three world-traveling children.

ABOUT FIVE STAR PUBLICATIONS

Linda F. Radke, veteran publisher and owner of Five Star Publications, has been ahead of her game since 1985—self-publishing before it was commonplace, partnership publishing before the rest of the world even knew what it was, and producing award-winning traditionally and nontraditionally published fiction and nonfiction for adults and children.

Five Star Publications produces premium quality books for clients and authors. Many have been recognized for excellence on local, national and international levels.

Linda also is author of *The Economical Guide to Self-Publishing* (a 2010 Paris Book Festival first-place winner in the "How-To" category and a Writer's Digest Book Club selection, now into its second edition) and *Promote Like a Pro: Small Budget, Big Show* (a Doubleday Executive Program Book Club selection). She is a founding member of the Arizona Book Publishing Association, was named "Book Marketer of the Year" by Book Publicists of Southern California, and received numerous public relations and marketing awards from Arizona Press Women.

Five Star Publications dedicates a percentage of profits to The Mark Foster Youth Fund and other charities chosen by the authors.

For more information about Five Star Publications, the Mark Foster Youth Fund, or charities supported by Five Star authors, visit www.FiveStarPublications.com.

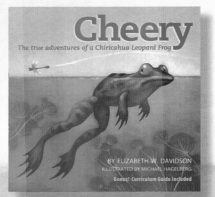

BY ELIZABETH W. DAVIDSON
ILLUSTRATED BY MICHAEL HAGELBERG
Bonus! Curriculum Guide Included

Cheery
The true adventures of a Chiricahua Leopard Frog

Cheery is a Chiricahua Leopard Frog.
He starts as an egg in a pond, turns
into a tadpole, and then into a frog.
Dr. Elizabeth W. Davidson explains why
Leopard Frogs and other amphibians might
become extinct. *Cheery: the true adventures of
a Chiricahua Leopard Frog* tells children what
can be done to save the frogs.

Publisher: Five Star Publications, Inc.
P.O. Box 6698, Chandler AZ 85246-6698
Price: $15.95 U.S. / Paperback / Nonfiction
Size: 8"x 8" / 40 pages
ISBN: 978-1-58985-025-5
Pub Date: Early 2011
Website: www.CheeryAFrogsTale.com

Item	Quantity	Unit price		
Cheery: the true adventures of a Chiricahua Leopard Frog		$15.95 US $16.95 CAN	Item total:	$
Add 8.8% sales tax on all orders originating in AZ:				$
Shipping–$6.50 for the first book and $1.00 for each additional book going to the same address. (US rates): Ground shipping only. Allow 1 to 2 weeks for delivery.				$
			TOTAL:	$

NAME:

ADDRESS:

CITY, STATE, ZIP:

DAYTIME PHONE: FAX:

EMAIL:

Method of payment:
❏ VISA   ❏ Mastercard   ❏ Discover   ❏ Amer.Express

Account Number:

Expiration Date:

Signature:

❏ I'm interested in having the author and/or illustrator visit my school. Please contact Linda Radke at 480-940-8182.
❏ Send a Five Star Catalog.
❏ Personalize signed copy. _____

Little
Five
Star

www.CheeryAFrogsTale.com

P.O. Box 6698 • Chandler, AZ 85246-6698
(480) 940-8182   866-471-0777   Fax: (480) 940-8787
info@FiveStarPublications.com   www.FiveStarPublications.com